WILDLY CUTE ANIMALS!

HEDGEHOGS

BY KRISTEN RAJCZAK NELSON

Gareth Stevens
PUBLISHING

Library of Congress Cataloging-in-Publication Data
Names: Rajczak Nelson, Kristen author
Title: Hedgehogs / Kristen Rajczak Nelson.
Description: Buffalo, New York : Gareth Stevens Publishing, [2026] | Series: Wildly cute animals! | Includes index. | Audience: Grades K-1
Identifiers: LCCN 2025003854 (print) | LCCN 2025003855 (ebook) | ISBN 9781482471212 (library binding) | ISBN 9781482471205 (paperback) | ISBN 9781482471229 (ebook)
Subjects: LCSH: Hedgehogs–Juvenile literature
Classification: LCC QL737.E753 R35 2026 (print) | LCC QL737.E753 (ebook) | DDC 599.33/2–dc23/eng/20250228
LC record available at https://lccn.loc.gov/2025003854
LC ebook record available at https://lccn.loc.gov/2025003855

Published in 2026 by
Gareth Stevens Publishing
2544 Clinton Street
Buffalo, NY 14224

Designer: Jeffrey Taylor
Editor: Kristen Nelson

Photo credits: Series art (tan background) Elena_Design/Shutterstock.com; Cover, p. 1 Rudolf_Prchlik/Shutterstock.com; p. 5 Oksana_Schmidt/Shutterstock.com; p. 7 Rudolf_Prchlik/Shutterstock.com; p. 9 Natasha Zakharova/Shutterstock.com; p. 11 Rudolf_Prchlik/Shutterstock.com; p. 13 Serenity Images23/Shutterstock.com; p. 15 Stanislavskyi/Shutterstock.com; p. 16 (inset) Protasov AN/Shutterstock.com; p. 17 Twisted Pixels/Shutterstock.com; p. 19 slowmotiongli/Shutterstock.com; p. 21 Elijus3000/Shutterstock.com.

Printed in the United States of America

CONTENTS

Boldface words appear in the glossary.

Meet the Hedgehog

Hedgehogs are wildly cute! They are small mammals, or animals that have backbones, hair, and feed milk to their young. Hedgehogs have big ears that hear well. They have a small **snout**. They can smell well too.

What It Looks Like

Hedgehogs can be white, brown, and even black. They have hair on their face, neck, and belly. A hedgehog's back is covered in quills. Quills are made of keratin. This is what your hair and fingernails are made of too.

QUILLS

Get to Know Quills

Quills are hard. The ends are pointy. When a hedgehog gets scared, its quills rise up. It tucks its head, legs, and tail in. It makes itself into a spiky ball! This **protects** it from being eaten by **predators**.

Where in the Wild

There are around 15 different kinds of hedgehog. They are found in the wild across Europe, Asia, and Africa. They can live in many different **habitats**. They live in **deserts**, forests, and even people's backyards!

Nesting

Some hedgehogs make nests on the ground. They use sticks, leaves, and dead grass. Others use their **claws** to dig burrows. Hedgehogs live in burrows left by other animals too. Those that live in the desert may dig under the sand to stay cool.

Awake at Night

Hedgehogs are nocturnal. That means they sleep during the day. They are most active at night. They may curl up in a ball to sleep. Then, they look for food when night falls.

What's for Dinner?

All hedgehogs eat **insects**. Some eat other animals too, such as slugs and snails. Hedgehogs that live in the deserts of Africa may eat dead snakes and scorpions! Hedgehogs may eat fruit, grass, and seeds as well.

SCORPION

Hedgie Families

Hedgehogs like to be alone. They only pair up to have babies. Mothers may have between one and eleven babies at a time. Babies are commonly called hoglets. They stay with their mom for a month or more.

Good Pet?

Some people think the cute hedgehog is a great pet. They are easy to care for. However, they are not allowed to be kept as pets in some places in the United States, including California and Washington, DC.

GLOSSARY

claw: An animal's sharp nail.

desert: An area of land that gets very little rain.

habitat: The natural place where an animal lives.

insect: A small, often winged, animal with six legs and three main body parts.

predator: An animal that hunts and eats other animals.

protect: To keep safe.

snout: An animal's nose and mouth.

FOR MORE INFORMATION

BOOKS

Mallory, Louis. *Do You Want a Pet Hedgehog?* Buffalo, NY: Enslow Publishing, 2025.

Stewart, Melissa. *Summertime Sleepers: Animals that Estivate*. Watertown, MA: Charlesbridge, 2024.

WEBSITES

Everything About Hedgehog Pets
brookhavenanimalhosp.com/site/blog/2024/06/15/keeping-hedgehog-pet
Find out if a hedgehog is the right pet for you here.

Hedgehog | San Diego Zoo Animals
animals.sandiegozoo.org/animals/hedgehog
Read more about hedgehogs and see more cute pictures.

INDEX